Fire TV Stick
User Guide

User-Friendly Guide to Get the Most Out of Amazon Fire TV Stick

NOTES TO THE READER

Table of Contents

INTRODUCTION

The Amazon Fire TV is a streaming media player, which means it takes content from the Internet (videos, music, games, etc.) and displays it on your TV. The Fire TV comes in two models: the **Amazon Fire TV**, which is a small box and the **Fire TV Stick**. The two models work very similarly, but obviously there are some differences; otherwise, the stick wouldn't be $50 cheaper now, would it?!

Both models support 1080p HD resolution. The box also supports 4K Ultra HD.

The Fire TV box connects to your TV with an HDMI cable and plugs into the wall with a standard A/C adapter. The Fire TV Stick plugs directly into an HDMI port on your TV, which makes it great for wall-mounted TVs. The power comes from a USB cable that you can plug into a USB port on your TV or into the wall with the included adapter.

The box is faster and has more memory. It also has a port for connecting it to your router with an Ethernet cable and a USB port and microSD slot to provide additional storage, none of which the stick has.

The box has some extra apps that aren't supported by the stick (~5200 vs. 4800). I think these are mostly games that have higher performance requirements.

Not surprisingly, the Fire TV is very tightly integrated with the Amazon Instant Video service. But there are tons of other content providers that work with it including Netflix, Hulu, HBO GO and HBO NOW, Sling TV, ESPN, Disney, PBS, History, YouTube, NBA, and much more.

Buying an Amazon Fire TV does not give you access to the content you can watch on it, just like buying a TV does not give you access to cable TV shows. You need to have accounts with each service that provides the content (some free, some paid) and/or subscribe to a cable/satellite package that gives you permission to access shows from specific networks through the Fire TV. When you see an app listed as "free" on the Fire TV interface or the Amazon website, it just means there's no cost to install the app itself on your player. It has nothing to do with whether the content accessed by the app costs money.

The Fire TV supports lots of music services as well,

including their own Amazon Music, Pandora, Spotify, and iHeart Radio.

There are free and paid games available for both devices, including highly popular ones like Crossy Road, Candy Crush Saga, and Minecraft. Additionally, there's a **Fire TV Gaming Edition**, which has a full-on console so you can play more complex games.

If you have a compatible Kindle Fire tablet or Android device, you can duplicate your screen on your TV. This has a couple of benefits:

- Any streaming media you can access via your compatible device you can now watch on your TV—for example, you can watch shows from broadcast and cable networks this way if the network streams them on their websites or through mobile apps that don't have built-in Fire TV support.
- You can also see any non-streaming content from your tablet or phone on your TV. Maybe you want to scroll through your Twitter feed on a large screen or access your email or browse match.com

profiles—anything you're doing on the device will display on your TV.

CHAPTER 1: FIRE TV STICK HARDWARE BASICS

The Fire TV Stick includes a micro-USB port (for power only) and an HDMI connector. The HDMI connector goes directly into your TV or into the included HDMI extender.

Note: Fire TV Stick only supports HDMI output

USB Cable and Power Adapter USB Cable connects your Fire TV Stick to a power source. Plug one end of the cable into the micro-USB port on your Fire TV Stick and the other end into the included power adapter and a power outlet. You can also plug the USB cable into a USB port on your TV for power, but use the included power adapter and plug it into a power outlet is recommended for optimal performance. The USB port can't be used to connect Fire TV Stick to computers or other devices. To turn off Fire TV Stick, unplug the USB cable from the device or from the power source.

Note: It is not necessary to turn off Fire TV Stick when you are finished using it. Your Fire TV Stick is designed to conserve energy by going into sleep mode after 30 minutes while continuing to automatically receive important software updates.

HDMI Extender Cable The HDMI extender is included with your Fire TV Stick and can be used to ensure your Fire TV Stick fits securely into your TV. The HDMI extender may also improve your Wi-Fi connection. To use the HDMI extender, plug the Fire TV Stick into the HDMI extender, and then plug the HDMI extender into an available HDMI port on your TV.

CHAPTER 2: NAVIGATE YOUR AMAZON FIRE TV DEVICE

Use your compatible remote to access the Home screen and your movies, TV shows, games, and apps. Press the 5-way directional trackpad to move up, down, left, or right. Press the middle Select button to select a content item, function, or category.

To do this... Try this...

Go to the Home screen

Press the Home button.

Return to the previous screen

Press the Back button.

Select a movie, TV show, game, or app

Press the middle Select button.

Wake up your Amazon Fire TV device Press any button to wake up your Amazon Fire TV device. Your Amazon Fire TV device goes into sleep mode after 30 minutes of inactivity or shows the screen saver according to your screen saver settings.

Put your Amazon Fire TV device to Sleep Your Amazon Fire TV device goes into sleep mode after 30 minutes of inactivity. However, you can manually put the device into Sleep mode: From the Home screen, go to Settings > System > Sleep.

Tip: Quickly access various features with the Quick Access Menu. To open it, press and hold the Home button on your Amazon remote.

Access purchased movies, TV shows, games, and apps From the Home screen, select one of the following options from the Main Menu:

• Video Library - Your purchased or rented Amazon Instant Video movies and TV shows.

Note: Movies and TV shows from third-party apps, such as Netflix and Hulu, are only accessible directly from the apps, not the Video Library.

• Games - Your purchased games appear in Your Games Library.

• Apps - Your purchased apps appear in Your Apps Library.

• Music - Purchased, imported, and Prime content added to your library will appear in Your Music Library.

Remove content from the Home screen To remove an item from the Recent carousel, navigate to the item, and then select Remove from Recent.

To do this... Try this...

To remove a title from Recommended Movies and TV, navigate to the item, and then select Not Interested.

Change the screen saver settings From the Home screen, select Settings > System > Screen Saver. Update the screen saver slide style, slide speed, start time, and photo album.

Turn off your Amazon Fire TV device To turn off your Amazon Fire TV device, unplug the power cord from the back of the device or from the wall outlet. You can also put the device into Sleep mode: From the Home screen, go to Settings > System > Sleep.

Note: You don't need to turn off the Amazon Fire TV device when you are finished using it. It will go into sleep mode after 30 minutes while continuing to automatically receive important software updates. On Amazon Fire TV, the LED indicator on the front of the device will turn off when the device is in sleep mode.

CHAPTER 3: MAIN MENU BASICS

The Home screen includes the Main Menu, which allows you to access your account and device settings, along with movie, TV show, game, and app content libraries.

Press the Home button on the remote to return to the Home Screen and Main Menu options.

Main Menu option Description Search for movies, TV shows, games, apps, music, and music videos from Vevo. Use the remote to search for content titles using voice input or an onscreen keyboard.

Home Review content recommendations and recent activity. Recent - Your recently viewed movies, TV shows, games, Cloud Drive photos/videos, or apps. To remove an item from Recent, navigate to the item and then select Remove from Recent. Featured Movies & TV or Apps & Games - Timely and relevant promotions featured by Amazon and other content providers. You cannot remove items from the Featured listings. Other Movies, TV, Apps & Games – Automated listings that include Amazon's newest (New Releases, Recently

Added to Prime), best (Top Movies, Free Games), or recommended content (Recommended Movies, Recommended TV). You can only remove items from the Recommended Movies and TV listings.

Prime Video If you are an Amazon Prime member, you can quickly and easily browse the Prime Instant Video library and watch movies and TV shows in this category at no extra cost.

Movies Rent, buy and watch movies from the Amazon Instant Video store and some other installed video apps. If you are an Amazon Prime member, you can quickly and easily browse the Prime Instant Video library and watch movies and TV shows in this category at no extra cost.

TV Buy and watch TV show episodes or seasons from the Amazon Instant Video store and some other installed video apps. If you are an Amazon Prime member, you can quickly and easily browse the Prime Instant Video library and watch movies and TV shows in this category at no extra cost.

Watchlist Access your Amazon Instant Video Watchlist. Your Watchlist is a list of movies or TV shows you want to buy,

Main Menu Option Description

Rent, or watch later. After you buy or rent the movie or TV show, it is available to stream from your Video Library.

Video Library Your Video Library includes all of the Amazon Instant Video movies and TV shows you've purchased or are currently renting but does not include the movies, and TV shows that you've watched through Prime Instant Video. The content you purchase is stored in the Cloud and available to stream to your device. Movies and TV shows from third-party apps, such as Netflix and Hulu, are only accessible directly from the apps, not the Video Library.

FreeTime (only available on Amazon Fire TV) Set up and manage Amazon FreeTime profiles from your Amazon Fire TV. Amazon FreeTime allows you to create up to four personalized profiles for your children to access videos, apps, and games that you selected for them.

Games Shop for, buy and play games from the Amazon Appstore. Use your Amazon GameCircle profile to view and compare achievements, leaderboards, and time played in a game. You can pair Amazon Fire or Bluetooth game controllers with your device.

Apps Shop for and buy games and apps from the Amazon Appstore. Movies and TV shows available through third- party apps, such as Netflix and Hulu, can be accessed through those apps in the Apps menu.

Music Browse and stream the music from Your Amazon Music Library, including songs you purchased from the Digital Music Store or imported to Your Music Library. Listen to Prime Music that you added to you library from another device. While listening to songs on your Amazon Fire TV device, X-Ray for Music displays the lyrics so you can follow along, if available.

Note: You will only be able to play Prime music that has been added to your library from a computer or another compatible device, such as the Amazon Music app on your phone or your Fire Tablet. You cannot add new Prime Music from your Amazon Fire TV device.

Photos Access photos and personal videos from your Amazon Cloud Drive account. You can also start photo slideshows and set individual photos as screen savers.

Settings View and manage your Amazon Fire TV device apps, controllers, parental controls, Internet connection, and more.

CHAPTER 4: SETTINGS BASICS

Your Amazon Fire TV device is designed to make most configuration settings automatic, but you can use the Settings menu to further manage your apps, Internet connection, controllers, screen savers, and more. From the Home screen, select Settings.

Tip: You can quickly access Settings by pressing and holding the Home button on your remote or on the most recent version of the Fire TV Remote App.

Setting Description Display and Sounds Set a screensaver, configure the display, mirror a compatible device, and manage audio settings. Second Screen Notifications Enable discovery of Amazon Instant Video playback and Photos on Amazon Fire TV device from nearby compatible mobile devices.

(FreeTime &) Parental Controls Enable or disable Amazon FreeTime, which allows you to create a personalized profile for your child to access videos, apps, and games that you selected for them. Parental Controls restrict purchasing, content types, and access to other features. On Amazon Fire TV, enable or disable Amazon FreeTime, which allows you to create a personalized profile for your child to access videos, apps, and games that you selected for them. Amazon FreeTime is not available on Fire TV Stick.

Note: Parental Controls will not restrict content in third-party applications. Parental controls for third-party applications are determined by the app provider.

Controllers and Bluetooth Devices Add, unpair, or update remotes and Bluetooth game controllers. View paired remote apps and third party remotes. Go to Fire TV Remote App Basics on page 30 to learn how to pair and update the Fire TV Remote App. Add and unpair supported Bluetooth accessories, such as headphones. Go to Connect a Bluetooth Accessory to Your Amazon Fire TV for more information.

Applications

• Manage Amazon GameCircle, Appstore, and install application settings.

• Enable or disable GameCircle nickname sharing, Whispersync for Games, Appstore automatic updates, and in-app purchases.

• Force stop, clear data, clear cache, or uninstall downloaded applications.

Setting Description

Note: If you clear data, the app will not be deleted; however, your saved information, such as game scores, may be lost.

System

• Put your Amazon Fire TV device to sleep

• Restart your device

• View device information

• Manage USB Storage (Amazon Fire TV only)

• Change network or time zone settings

• Disable app notifications (Quiet Time)

• Check for software updates

• Factory reset your device

Help Access help videos, quick tips, and Amazon customer service information.

My Account Register or Deregister your Amazon Fire TV device with your Amazon account. You can also select Sync Amazon Content to make sure your latest content purchases are available on your device.

CHAPTER 5: REGISTER OR DEREGISTER YOUR AMAZON FIRE TV DEVICE

In order to use your Amazon Fire TV device, register it to your Amazon account. To register your device, connect it to the Internet. To learn more, go to Set Up a Wireless or Wired Connection on page 45. If you purchased your Amazon Fire TV device online from Amazon using your Amazon account, it should already be registered to you. If you purchased your Amazon Fire TV device from another retailer or received it as a gift, follow the on-screen instructions for entering your Amazon account information and password. To verify that your Amazon Fire TV device is registered to your Amazon account:

From the Home screen, select Settings > My Account.

• If no account is currently registered, select Register to register your Amazon Fire TV device to the desired Amazon account.

• If you would like to register a different Amazon account, select the Amazon account that is currently registered, and then select deregister.

CHAPTER 6: ACCESS AND REMOVE CONTENT

Your Amazon Fire TV device can access Amazon and third-party apps, games, music, videos, and more, which are referred to as "content" throughout our Help pages. There are several ways to access and remove content from your Amazon Fire TV device. To find content, such as movies, TV shows, games, and apps, select a content type from the Main Menu on the Home screen.

To access... Do this...

Prime Instant Video Movies & TV shows Navigate to the Recently Added Prime Movies & TV or Top Prime Movies or TV listings. If you are a Prime member and a movie or TV show is eligible for Prime Instant Video, select the artwork of the video to watch it at no additional cost.

Amazon Instant Video purchases or rentals From the Home screen, select Video Library. Your Video Library includes all the Amazon Instant Video movies and TV shows you've purchased and all active rentals. Once a rental period has expired, you will no longer see the video in your Video Library.

Amazon Instant Videos to buy, rent, or watch later From the Home screen, select Watchlist. Your Watchlist is a list of Amazon Instant Video movies or TV shows you want to buy, rent, or watch later. After you buy or rent the movie or TV show, it is also available from your Video Library.

Note: Content from third-party apps, such as Netflix and Hulu, cannot be added to your Watchlist or Video Library.

Music From the Home screen, select Music to access all of the music in your Amazon Music Library.

Note: You cannot browse or add Prime Music to your collection with your Amazon Fire TV device. Add Prime Music to your collection from the Amazon Music app on a supported device. You can also go to www.amazon.com/ prime music to add Prime Music to your library.

Game Purchases from the Home screen, select Games. Your purchased games appear in Your Games Library. Your Games Library includes all the games you purchased from the Amazon Appstore.

App Purchases from the Home screen, select Apps. Your purchased apps appear in Your Apps Library. Your Apps Library includes all the apps you purchased from the Amazon Appstore.

Remove Content from Your Amazon Fire TV Device

If you have content that you no longer use, you can remove items from your Amazon Fire TV device. Any purchases made from Amazon are saved to the Cloud and can be downloaded again to your device.

Note: Individual app settings or in-app items may be lost when removed from your Amazon Fire TV device.

To remove content from... Do this...

Watchlist from Watchlist, navigate to a movie or TV show and then select Remove from Watchlist.

Recently Watched sections From Movies or TV, navigate to a movie or TV show and then select the Remove from Recently Watched.

Video Library You cannot remove content from your Video Library using Amazon Fire TV device. The content you purchase is stored in the Cloud and can only be removed from Manage Your Content and Devices (Amazon.com full site).

Recent carousel On the Home screen, you'll see personalized recommendations in the Recent section. The listings that display are based on your recent activity. To remove an item, navigate to the item and then select Remove from Recent.

Note: You cannot remove Featured or Top content on the Home screen.

CHAPTER 7: REMOTE BASICS

Your Amazon Fire TV device includes a wireless remote with a 5-way directional trackpad that allows you to quickly and easily navigate your device. Before you can use the remote, you must install the 2 AAA batteries (included) and pair it with your Amazon Fire TV device. To pair a third party remote, go to Connect a Bluetooth Accessory to Your Amazon Fire TV. Controls and performance may vary.

Amazon Fire TV Voice Remote (Front)

Included with Amazon Fire TV.

Amazon Fire TV Voice Remote (Back) To insert the 2 AAA batteries into the Amazon Fire TV Voice Remote:

1. Rotate the Fire TV Remote, so the top edge is facing downwards.

2. Apply pressure on the indent of the battery door and slide upwards.

Note: It can take a considerable amount of pressure to open the battery door.

3. Pull away the battery door and insert 2 AAA batteries.

4. Slide the door back into place and push in to secure.

Button Description

Voice Only available on the Amazon Fire TV Voice Remote

Search for movies, TV shows, games, or apps using voice commands. Voice search uses two built-in microphones to search for items using your voice commands.

Directional Navigation

• Press right to move to the right on your TV screen. Moving to the right from the Main Menu allows you to access the content libraries or storefronts such as movies, TV, games, apps, photos, and more.

• Press left to move to the left on your TV screen. Moving to the left allows you to return to the Main Menu from any content library or storefront.

• Press up to move up and press down to move down.

Select an item, function, or category.

Home Returns you to the Home screen from any screen on your Amazon Fire TV device.

Tip: Quickly access various features with the Quick Access Menu. To open it, press and hold the Home button on your Amazon remote.

Menu Presents various functions and settings depending on which screen you are accessing.

Back Returns you to the previous screen or action.

Rewind

Play/pause

Fast Forward

Media control buttons let you rewind, play, pause, and fast-forward video. Press the rewind or forward button once to skip 10 seconds backward or forward. Press and hold the rewind or forward button to continue navigating backward or forward in the video. Additional presses allow you to cycle through the available speed options.

CHAPTER 8: COMPATIBLE REMOTES FOR AMAZON FIRE TV DEVICES

You can control your Amazon Fire TV device with any of these remotes:

• Amazon Fire TV Voice Remote

• Amazon Fire TV Remote

• Fire TV Remote App on Fire phone, Fire Tablets, iOS devices (7.0 and higher) and Android devices (4.0 and higher)

• Amazon Fire Game Controller (sold separately)

• USB or Bluetooth keyboard

• Some third party Bluetooth game controllers

• Some third-party Bluetooth remotes

• Some third-party wireless USB receivers/remotes.

CHAPTER 9: GAME CONTROLLER BASICS

The Amazon Fire Game Controller (sold separately) is a wireless game controller that can be used to play games and access GameCircle with your Amazon Fire TV device. The Amazon Fire Game Controller can also be used as a remote, allowing you to access your movies, TV shows, games, and apps. Before you can use the Amazon Fire Game Controller, you must install 2 AA batteries and pair it with your Amazon Fire TV device. As soon as you install the 2 AA batteries, the controller is immediately "discoverable" on your Amazon Fire TV. If your Amazon Fire Game Controller isn't discovered, press the Home button on the controller for at least five seconds, and then release it.

Note: The Amazon Fire Game Controller is not shipped with Amazon Fire TV devices and is not compatible with all games.

To see which controllers are compatible with a game, navigate to a game and then select More Info. On the overview page, you'll find the controller information in the Works With box. When searching for games and apps, you can also filter the search results by:

Fire TV Remote

• Tablet Games on Fire TV

• Fire TV Game Controller

• Fire TV Stick (only visible on Fire TV Stick). Many third-party Bluetooth game controllers work with Amazon Fire TV devices.

Button Description

Home Returns you to the Home screen from any screen on Amazon Fire TV.

Amazon GameCircle Access your GameCircle dashboard while in a game, or access your Games Library.

Menu View and manage your Amazon Fire TV apps, controllers, and more.

Play / Pause / Fast Forward / Rewind Y, X, A, B Left and right shoulder and trigger buttons

These buttons are mainly used for gaming. Their specific features may change depending on the game being played. Tablet Games on Fire TV: These games require an Amazon Fire Game Controller or an Xbox

360 controller with a wireless USB receiver to be played.

• Left Joystick: Move "mouse" pointer

• A button: A single tap or click

• B button: Back (if available)

• Left shoulder button: Decrease cursor speed

• Right shoulder button: Increase cursor speed

Status Lights LED indicators at the front of the controller light up when the remote is on to indicate what player number the controller has been assigned (if the game uses player numbers).

CHAPTER 10: FIRE TV REMOTE APP BASICS

Use the Fire TV Remote App as an alternate way to navigate and use voice search on your Amazon Fire TV device. Before you use the Fire TV Remote App, connect the device with the app to the same Wi-Fi network as your Amazon Fire TV device and pair the app with your device.

To Do This... Try This Voice search

1. Press and hold the Voice icon at the top of the screen, then drag down. Don't release the icon until you're done speaking.

2. Say keywords related to the content items you want to search for (such as the title or genre).

Navigate menu items and categories To move the selection...

• Up: Swipe from the middle to the top

• Down: Swipe from the middle to the bottom

• Left: Swipe from the middle to the left

• Right: Swipe from the middle to the right

• Scroll: Swipe and hold to a specific direction

Select an item Tap the device screen

Use navigation options:

Home

Menu

Back

At the bottom of the screen, tap any of the navigation icons.

Tip: Quickly access various features with the Quick Access Menu. To open it, press and hold the Home button on your Amazon remote.

Make sure you are on the latest version of the Fire TV Remote App.

Enter text with a keyboard (may not be available in third-party apps, such as Netflix)

1. Select the keyboard icon in the top right corner of the screen.

2. Enter text.

3. Tap Done to close the keyboard.

Access media controls:

Rewind

Play/pause

1. Swipe up from the bottom of the screen.

2. Select Rewind, Pause, or Skip.

To Do This... Try This Fast Forward

Note: The Fire TV Remote App is not designed to play games. Some games might work, but performance will vary. The app does not currently support Second Screen or Display Mirroring. For more information, go to Use an Amazon Fire TV Device with a Second

Screen Device on page 51 and Use an Amazon Fire TV Device as a Display Mirroring Destination on page 50.

CHAPTER 11: DOWNLOAD & PAIR THE FIRE TV REMOTE APP

Download the Fire TV Remote App to your compatible mobile device and pair it with your Amazon Fire TV device to use it as an alternate remote. Compatibility, The Fire TV Remote App, is available on:

• Amazon Fire phone

• Fire Tablets (with a microphone)

• Android 4.0 or higher

• iOS 7.0 or higher The app is compatible with Amazon Fire TV on software version 1.4.1 or higher. It is also compatible with Fire TV Stick. If you use advanced settings on your router, you must enable Multicast support to use the Fire TV Remote App. Contact your router manufacturer for details. Download The app is available for download at these locations:

• Amazon Appstore

• Apple Store

• Google Play Store To download the Fire TV Remote App, go to your preferred app store from any compatible device and search for "Amazon Fire TV Remote App." Follow the onscreen instructions to complete the installation. Pair To pair the Fire TV Remote App with your Amazon Fire TV device:

1. Connect to the same Wi-Fi network as your Amazon Fire TV device. 2. Launch the app and select the Amazon Fire TV device you want to pair with. 3. In the app, enter the code that is displayed on your TV screen. The app is now paired.

To see all of the remote apps that are paired with your Amazon Fire TV device, go to Settings > Controllers and Bluetooth Devices > Fire TV Remotes.

Note: Once you pair the Fire TV Remote App with your Amazon Fire TV device, you cannot unpair it. However, if you factory reset your Amazon Fire TV device, all paired devices will be removed. To block access to a paired device, you can also change your Wi-Fi network password.

CONCLUSION

The Amazon Fire TV Stick is the bargain version of Amazon's super-fast voice search-enabled Fire TV. The HDMI version certainly sacrifices a lot of things that make Fire TV great, but is that bargain worth it? Absolutely.

Enter the Fire TV Stick, Amazon's $40 stripped-down answer to the higher-end streaming box. Like the Roku Stick or Chromecast, it pops into the HDMI port on the back of your TV and opens your boob tube to a whole new world of streaming content. It's just a little bit clunkier than its Fire predecessor. The remote loses its matte finish and just feels a little more plasticity. The HDMI port comes with a power cable, and an extender if you need it.

Where specs are concerned, it's basically half of a Fire TV box—it has 1GB of memory, a dual-core processor, and a cheaper remote that doesn't come with voice search. But that's not to say voice search doesn't work with the Fire. You can use voice search with the stick, you just need the remote app, which only exists on Android for now, or you'll need to buy the more expensive $30 remote that normally comes standard with the Fire TV box. Which, once you're spending a total of $70, you might as well just bite the bullet and pay $30 more for the whole kit and caboodle and two more cores worth of oomph.

In any case, if you're not used to Amazon's excellent voice search, you won't miss it. If you are, you will. I did! Fire TV is my default streaming box.

I love it for the things I've mentioned above, and even though in my house, I have a few options from which to stream stuff (Roku Stick, Roku 3, Xbox, and the horror show that is a default Samsung Smart TV interface), I always, always default to Fire TV. Besides what I've already discussed in terms of speed and search, Fire TV just offers up a really nice interface. Nice how? Nice to look at, nice to navigate, and simple to understand.

On the left-hand side you have your categories (apps, Prime video, music, photos, etc.), and when you select one, you can search within that section. You have your pick of apps, which includes almost everything you could want (Netflix, Spotify, Showtime, YouTube, Vimeo, and so forth), except for HBO Go. And apparently, that one's coming—eventually.

But the best reason to go with a Fire TV is if you want movies and shows from Amazon. Because of Amazon Amazon Amazon. No, really, that's what we always argue about the Bezos Universe. It has content on its side. And Fire TV banks on that in a beautiful way. The system is connected to your Amazon account, so even if something *isn't* included on Prime Instant Video, you can just click and click and pay to watch *Groundhog Day* or what-have-you. It's comfortable and easy TV-watching. You don't have to think! That's not a bad thing.

All of that stays the same with Fire TV Stick. It's just in a different package.

So the question a lot of people have is how does Fire TV Stick stack up to Chromecast? They're similar in terms of what they do (stream content), what they cost ($39 and $35 respectively), and what they are (HDMI sticks). Fire TV just does it a little bit better, thanks to a couple of convenience factors, one being a remote. Chromecast must rely on your phone, tablet, or computer in order to cast stuff to your television, and that works just fine for some. But others? Others just want a dang remote. That's what we've become used to since we started using TVs. "Where's the clicker?" Every dad asks in living rooms around the world on Sunday afternoons. We want it. We need it. It reassures us.

www.ingramcontent.com/pod-product-compliance
Lightning Source LLC
Chambersburg PA
CBHW071300280526
45788CB00004B/1784